Original title:
Life: The Question, The Answer, and the Snack

Copyright © 2025 Creative Arts Management OÜ
All rights reserved.

Author: Cameron Blair
ISBN HARDBACK: 978-1-80566-198-6
ISBN PAPERBACK: 978-1-80566-493-2

Sips of Solace

With a cup of cheer, I ponder
What's the secret sauce for hunger?
Is it wisdom brewed in laughter,
Or a snack that comes after?

The Dessert of Dreams

Chocolate whispers, sweet delight,
Pie in the skies, a tasty sight.
What if dreams were served on trays,
With sprinkles of sunshine, in glorious ways?

Sauces of the Soul

Ketchup on questions, mustard on hopes,
Tangled in flavors, like endless ropes.
Dip in the spicy, the zesty advance,
What's your flavor? Come take a chance!

Stirring the Pot of Philosophy

In a pot of thoughts, I stir and muse,
What are the snacks I must choose?
Is the answer a cookie or maybe a cake,
Or the giggles that rise when we bake?

Sipping the Sips of Sage

In the cup, a mystic brew,
With hints of laughter, not so few.
A sip brings thought, a giggle's kick,
What's the meaning? Just take a lick.

The leaves whisper tales profound,
Of silly things that laugh abound.
As I ponder with my mug,
A frothy cloud's a gentle hug.

Bakery of Questions

In a shop where dough is spun,
Each question baked, a tasty pun.
A muffin holds the world's great whys,
While cookies chuckle with surprise.

The oven hums, the pastries rise,
With flaky crusts and sweet replies.
A pie that's shaped like a frown,
Turns upside down, oh me, oh wow!

The Feast of Answers

Gather round for bites of truth,
In salad greens and cakes of youth.
A plate of wisdom, served with glee,
Each forkful asks, "What's funny, see?"

With every dish, a hearty laugh,
In mashed potatoes, I find a path.
Spiced with joy, a zesty cheer,
The answer's clear, it's all right here.

Flavorful Deliberations

Seated at the table of thought,
With snacks and queries, a tangled knot.
Chips and dip, they spell delight,
As I munch, the ideas ignite.

In every crunch, a question springs,
The salsa dances, inspiration sings.
With nachos layered, bold and bright,
Tasty debates continue all night.

Essence in Every Bite

In a world where crumbs do dance,
Each snack holds a hidden chance.
A chip may whisper secrets deep,
While cookies promise dreams in sleep.

The mustard's bold, the ketchup's sweet,
In every taste, life's rhythms beat.
A simple bite can change the game,
Just one more chip, they chant my name.

Popcorn pops like questions bright,
With buttered answers, oh so right.
A slice of pizza, cheesy bliss,
In every morsel, laughter's kiss.

So gather 'round, let's make a feast,
With every crunch, our joy released.
For in this meal, we find delight,
Chasing worries with every bite.

Questions with Sprinkles

What's the flavor of a good debate?
Is it salty tears or sweeten fate?
With sprinkles bright, we toss our fears,
As donuts make the laughter clear.

Is the universe a bowl of cake?
Where layers hide what we can't fake?
Each frosting swirl a twist of fate,
While cupcakes wait to celebrate.

In every crunch and slurp, we find,
The silly answers that rewind.
Soda bubbles lift our souls,
As pie reminds us of our goals.

So here's a slice of mystery,
With sprinkles on our history.
Let's dive into the unknown glee,
With every question, boundless spree.

The Symphony of Sustenance

Listen closely, hear the fry,
Sizzling truths and buttery lies.
Each spatula strikes a chord of cheer,
In the kitchen, all our dreams appear.

Tacos flutter like whispers sweet,
Encasing wonders in every bite to eat.
With salsa melodies that dance and play,
While nachos echo, 'Stay and stay!'

A cookie crumbles, laughter rings,
In this symphony, joy springs.
As pasta twirls in a whimsical tune,
We twirl our forks beneath the moon.

So gather 'round, let's share our voice,
In this feast, come rejoice!
For every meal's a show to see,
With food as our sweet harmony.

Gathering Around the Table

Around the table, chatter flows,
With laughter shared, the absurdity grows.
A stew of stories, thick and hearty,
As cookies crash this dinner party.

Who knew a salad could spark the fun?
With dressing drizzles, jokes weigh a ton.
We pass the bread like a strange riddle,
Guessing why the butter's middle.

The dessert table's a sight to behold,
With mysteries wrapped in sugar and gold.
Each scoop whispers culinary dreams,
While ice cream swirls in playful schemes.

So lift a fork and raise a cheer,
For every meal brings more than near.
In every bite, new tales are spun,
And laughter makes the world run.

Questions Served Hot

Why does toast always land face down?
The butter's slick, it makes me frown.
Is cereal soup? Should I debate?
With milk as a friend, it's never too late.

Why do socks vanish in the wash?
It's a mystery that makes me nosh.
Are cats plotting a secret scheme?
While I chase dreams, they steal my cream.

Can a sandwich truly be a meal?
With chips on the side, what's the deal?
Are pickles fruits or veggies, pray?
I've got hungry thoughts, what do you say?

Is a burrito a wrapped hug?
A warm, savory, happy mug.
With laughter served on a silver tray,
Dine on these musings, and laugh away!

Conundrums in a Cup

Why does coffee feel like a friend?
It perks me up and helps me mend.
Can a donut's hole be called a seat?
For munching thoughts, it can't be beat.

Is water just the universe's tease?
Or a simple drink to cool the breeze?
Do fries make everything feel alright?
I munch and ponder, day and night.

Is tea a hug in a cozy mug?
Or a potion meant to give a shrug?
Do we need answers, or just some snacks?
As we question, where are the cracks?

With every sip, a thought to stew,
In this cup, I find my clue.
Life's little puzzles all arise,
With wit and munchies, let's be wise!

Edible Epics

What's the meaning of a wobbly chair?
Does it dance to make us care?
Is pizza truly a round delight?
With every slice, I feel so bright.

Can cookies crumble under truth's weight?
Or do they giggle and celebrate?
Is spaghetti a tangled mystery?
Sauced in sauce, it's tasty history.

What if chips are a crunchy crutch?
A seasoned friend when life is much?
Do grapes gossip when turned to wine?
Or simply swirl in a fruity line?

Life's a buffet, with flavors bold,
In every question, stories unfold.
So grab a snack, and take a bite,
Munch on the antics, day or night!

The Spices of Self

Why is mustard always so bright?
A little tang brings wrongs to right.
Is garlic a vampire's worst dread?
Or a flavor that dances on the bread?

Are salads just a vegetable tease?
With croutons thrown as a tasty breeze?
Can pickles claim they're crunchy stars?
What do peppers think from their jars?

Do snacks giggle during the night?
As we savor, do they take flight?
Can chocolate solve all of the woes?
Each bite a burst where laughter grows.

The flavors swirl, a lively mix,
In every crunch, we find our tricks.
With spice and cheer in every shelf,
We nibble on truths of the self.

Messy Plates of Possibility

In kitchens bright, we crunch and munch,
Flavors collide, a merry bunch.
The pasta spills, the sauce takes flight,
Chaos reigns in this tasty plight.

With every bite, new dreams unfurl,
Forks do battle, as spices swirl.
Carrots dance, potatoes prance,
In this feast, we take a chance.

From grape to grain, all serve a role,
In messy plates, we find our goal.
Laughter bubbles like boiling stew,
Join the spread, there's enough for you!

As napkins fly, we raise a cheer,
For flavors bold and friends held dear.
Together we taste, together we play,
In this banquet of dreams, we share the day.

Noodles of Nostalgia

Twirl the noodles, memories rise,
A splash of laughter, a dash of sighs.
With every slurp, a tale we tell,
Of days gone by, where we all fell.

Spaghetti hugs and warmth so bright,
Sauces splatter, but feels so right.
From childhood bowls to grown-up feasts,
Each bite a story, laughter increased.

Chopsticks fumble, we all get stuck,
Using forks, oh what bad luck!
But every twirl brings smiles anew,
In noodles thick, we find our crew.

With flavors tangy and textures wild,
We're all just kids, free and reviled.
In the dance of forks, let's twirl once more,
For in these bowls, we all explore.

The Salad of Sentience

Crunchy thoughts in leafy greens,
Tossed around by silly means.
Carrots stick in, radishes pop,
In this bowl, we never stop.

With vinaigrette like questions posed,
Each garnish a truth, neatly enclosed.
We toss our dreams and mix our fears,
In salad bars, we shed our tears.

The croutons chatter, the olives smile,
They share their secrets in a while.
Dressing on thoughts, a flavor burst,
In this crunchy mess, we quench our thirst.

So forth we dine on thoughts so bright,
With every bite, we find delight.
In lettuce layers, a world awaits,
Join the feast before it vacates!

Dipping into Depth

Chips and guac, a perfect pair,
In bowls that hold our deepest fare.
With every dip, we seek and probe,
In salsa thick, we find our globe.

The crunch resounds like echoes past,
As stories flow, and laughter casts.
In creamy depths, our secrets swirl,
With every bite, our dreams unfurl.

Guacamole's wisdom, bold and bright,
Saves us all from the bland of night.
Friendship dips like chips in cheese,
Together we munch on thoughts with ease.

As bowls empty, our spirits rise,
In these shared snacks, we find our ties.
So dip anew in flavors grand,
In the art of sharing, together we stand.

The Snack That Sparked a Revelation

In the cupboard, a bag does gleam,
Potato chips whisper, 'Come dream!'
Crunch, crunch, the revelations roll,
Maybe snacks are the key to the soul!

Dip of guac, so rich and divine,
Every bite feels like a sign.
Who knew a snack could be the muse,
For pondering life's wild, crazy views?

A cookie crumbles, sends thoughts ablaze,
Are we just crumbs in a snack-filled maze?
Eating and thinking, it all intertwines,
In the pantry of thought, wisdom sometimes shines!

So here's to munching with curious bites,
Finding truth in those snack-filled nights.
For every crunch, a ponder to find,
The tasty snack that awakens the mind!

Between Chew and Contemplation

With each nibble, I pause and stare,
The meaning of everything hangs in the air.
A sandwich speaks, 'Take it slow!'
Between each bite, what do I know?

A pickle offers a sour reply,
As I ponder the munching of pie.
Do fries have wisdom, or just salt?
My thoughts get tangled in a doughnut vault.

Chewing my way through this ponderous feast,
Each taste brings the questions, at least.
A sip of soda gives it some flair,
What's fizz without thoughts that go somewhere?

So here I sit, half lost, half found,
Between each crunch, questions abound.
A life well-snacked is a life well-thought,
In the midst of bites, insight is sought!

Savory Reflections

In the kitchen, I slice and fry,
Each savory nibble draws thoughts nearby.
A steak declares, 'Chew longer, think deep!'
While pasta's wisdom is more for a sleep.

Oven-baked wonders smell of delight,
As I muse on snacks far into the night.
What does a jellybean know of love?
Such questions linger like sparrows above.

A muffin's warmth hugs me so tight,
Filling my mind with flavors so bright.
"Eat me first!" shouts the cake on the stand,
While thoughts diverge in crumbs, oh so grand!

Each savory bite, an eloquent play,
As I seek the meaning in what snacks may say.
With each taste, I chuckle and grin,
For profound thoughts may just come from within!

Bread Crumbs of Meaning

Around the loaf, I ponder and muse,
Each slice of wisdom, I choose to peruse.
What's the crust if the heart's all soft?
In the bakery of life, we're all aloft.

As breadcrumbs scatter the thoughts in the air,
I follow the trail, oh what's hiding there?
A buttered roll speaks of warmth and cheer,
"Don't weigh your thoughts, just enjoy the year!"

A baguette so long, it stretches the plot,
"Does my crust cover the depths that I've got?"
With every pull, a question outbraves,
While bready crumbs lead to countless saves!

So here's to the snacks, the giggles and grins,
In each simple crumb, the sage insight spins.
Eating my way through this whimsical riddle,
The answers are found in laughter and middle!

Snippets of Serenity

On a Monday morning, I sip my brew,
Wondering why the sun is still rising too.
A cat on the windowsill, stretching wide,
Chasing dreams of fish, with no place to hide.

The mailman arrives with a smile so bright,
His cargo of bills makes my wallet take flight.
But in his pocket, a snack sweet and round,
He offers me joy, and my worries are drowned.

A garden of thoughts blooms in my mind,
With patches of daisies, and some intertwined.
As I hop on a cloud, just me and my snack,
I'm suddenly wishing for pizza, not quack!

So here's to the snippets, so silly and small,
In moments of stillness, we cherish it all.
A giggle, a munch, under skies so vast,
We savor the present, 'cause future's a blast!

The Canvas of Existence

With crayons in hand, I paint my bright fate,
Mixing joy and chaos, like a pastry plate.
A splash of green laughter, with hints of despair,
The canvas of nonsense, but oh, how we care!

An apple on the table rolls off with a thunk,
It whispers sweet secrets, while I'm feeling funk.
I give it a nibble, it giggles right back,
The meaning of being, is snacking on snack!

Marshmallows float in my cup of hot tea,
They dance on the surface, just wild and free.
Between conversations with cupcakes and fries,
I seek out the truth, in their sugary skies.

So let's silly-paint life, with sprinkles and cream,
The masterpiece shown is not always a dream.
For in every bite, and in laughter's sweet song,
We find all the answers, where we all belong!

Craving Connection

In a crowded café, I spy a great croissant,
A buttery moment, oh yes, I do want!
With coffee in hand, I wave to a friend,
The chat is adventurous, like wishes we send.

We share all our secrets, both silly and deep,
Like why socks go missing, or why cats creep.
Each nibble to savor, each giggle to keep,
Life's a buffet table, a platter to reap!

The barista sings loudly, her apron's a sight,
She spins frozen yogurt, a delightful delight.
Between bites of doughnuts, my heart starts to race,
Friendship is seasoning, in this funny place.

So let's snack and connect, and smile with glee,
A dance on our taste buds, just you and just me.
In crumbs we discover, we're never alone,
Sharing every morsel brings warmth to the known!

Bread of Beliefs

With a loaf on the table, I ponder the air,
Is bread really sacred? It's yeast beyond compare!
A slice of conviction, a spread so divine,
Each crumb tells a story, in flavors we dine.

A buttered-up vision of dreams on my plate,
Munching on wisdom, oh how can I wait?
With a sprinkle of salt, to challenge the norm,
I toast to existence, and weather the storm.

In the world of snacks, each nibble a chance,
To bridge gaps of silence, invite a nice dance.
With pretzels of purpose and chips full of cheer,
I find all the meanings, tucked tightly in here.

So let's knead our beliefs, with laughter and glee,
In the dough of tradition, we'll always be free.
For the bread that we make, with our hearts full of grace,
Is a banquet of mirth, in this infinite space!

Digesting Dilemmas

In a world of choices vast,
Do I want this, or that? Oh, what a blast!
A cookie, a chip, a crunch to enjoy,
Decisions like snacks, oh what a ploy.

Should I sauté or should I bake?
Do I want pasta, or a sweet piece of cake?
With each nibble, a thought unfolds,
In flavors of wisdom, each bite bold.

The oven beeps, a joyful sound,
Do I flip, or let it spin around?
A recipe for laughter in every choice,
My tummy talks back, oh, hear its voice!

So I dine and I ponder, with glee in each bite,
Sometimes it's wrong, but hey, that's alright!
In every dilemma, I'll chuckle and snack,
For life's just a buffet, there's no looking back!

Flavorful Journeys

Where shall we roam in this feast of delight?
A taco truck here, a donut in sight.
Street carts aplenty, each with a grin,
Around every corner, new flavors begin.

With each tiny nibble, a story unfolds,
A journey of spices, of tales yet untold.
We'll dance with the mustard, the ketchup, the jam,
Together we feast, like a glorious fam!

Is it spicy or sweet? Do I dare to decide?
A plate full of questions, let's take them in stride.
Perhaps just a taste of each vibrant dish,
Each traveler's dream wrapped up in a swish.

So pack up your forks, your spoons, and your zest,
We're off to explore; it'll surely be best!
For every new flavor is an answer we seek,
A savory giggle, life's mystery's peak!

The Palette of Questions

A splash of confusion on a canvas so wide,
What drink pairs with fries? I ponder and glide.
A sip here, a crunch there, oh what a mess,
With colors of doubt, I try to express.

Paint it with nachos, or drizzle with cheese,
What toppings to choose? Oh, not with such ease!
With each little nib, I paint a bright hue,
Crafting my snacks like the great artists do.

Am I sweet like a cookie, or spunky like zest?
In the buffet of flavors, I simply can't rest.
Each question a flavor that dances on tongue,
In this art of the feast, oh, how we've sprung!

Let's swirl all our doubts on a platter of fun,
With each bite, a laugh, and the joy has begun.
So mix up your colors, don't stick to just one,
For the palette of snacks means we've all already won!

Savoring the Present

Take a bite of the future, a nibble of now,
Chewing on moments, oh, how to wow!
With cupcakes and giggles, we'll savor the day,
Each mouthful of joy leads us on our way.

A spoonful of laughter, a sprinkle of cheer,
What's better than sharing with friends gathered near?
From burgers to brownies, each taste a delight,
In this feast of the present, we munch till the night.

Don't fret about yesterday, let's relish in bliss,
What toppings to choose? Oh, let's not miss!
With bites full of joy, and laughter our side,
We'll toast to the moments, our hearts open wide.

So dig in, don't wait; don't waste even one crumb,
For savoring now is where all the fun comes!
With cookies and questions, we make memories last,
In this delightful banquet, we'll have a grand blast!

The Crumbs of Curiosity

Beneath the couch, the crumbs do hide,
A cookie trail, my snacky guide.
Questions linger, oh what to munch?
Is it cake? Is it pie? I'll take a bunch!

Each bite I ponder, is this the key?
To solve the riddle of snacks and glee?
Perhaps the answer's layered with cream,
Or simply a scoop of vanilla dream!

I chase my thoughts like crumbs on the floor,
Are snacks a delight, or a cosmic lore?
Plates piled high, my heart takes flight,
In this food quest, I'll dine all night!

So here I am, a curious chap,
In a snack-filled world, I take a nap.
With cookies, cakes, and chips on hand,
I ask the universe, but I'm just a fan!

In Search of Sweet Resolve

With chocolate bars stacked on the shelf,
I wonder if it's wise to think for myself.
The candy aisle calls with a festive cheer,
As I ponder life's meaning over root beer!

The gummy bears dance, so gleefully bright,
Is happiness here, hidden from sight?
Or is it found in the crunch of a chip,
Savoring flavors with each little dip?

Strawberry tarts, shortcake delight,
I question the answer deep into the night.
What's better than sweets at the end of the day?
A chocolate fountain, or lemon meringue play!

So here I sit with a bowl in my lap,
In search of the truth, while taking a nap.
The sweet resolve may be closer than thought,
A sugar-coated mystery, deliciously sought!

Pondering in the Kitchen

In my kitchen, I twist and turn,
With spatula in hand, my mind starts to burn.
Do carrots talk when left in the pot?
Or does the broccoli plot a vegetable plot?

A whisk in the air, I ponder the fate,
Of cookies and brownies, oh isn't that great?
Do they feel joy when I take a bite?
Or are they sad until my snack's in sight?

Flour on my shirt, I giggle with glee,
As thoughts of the pantry dance just for me.
Like a detective, I mix and I mash,
Searching for snacks in a kitchen flash!

The oven's preheated, my snacks are in line,
Are they my answers? I guess they're divine.
With bites of delight, I bite to explore,
The mysteries of snacks, forever I'll adore!

Whispers of What Comes Next

The cookie jar whispers, 'What will you choose?'
Should I munch on a muffin or go for a snooze?
Questions arise as the kettle begins,
Does tea really know where sweet humor spins?

Glimpses of snacks dance 'round my head,
What if I mix chocolate and bread?
The toaster chuckles, 'Give it a try!'
While pancakes flip as if they could fly!

A sprinkle of salt, a dash of delight,
Answers are brewing in meals every night.
Nutty granola and fruits in a bowl,
Is this where I find the meaning of soul?

With crumbs by my side, I question and snack,
Life's mysteries unfold with each tasty track.
So bring on the snacks, let the fun begin,
In this world of treats, I'll always fit in!

Banquets of Bonding

Gather round the table, all laugh and jest,
Tales of old mishaps, who thinks they're the best?
Pasta flops and curry spills, food flying through the air,
We toast to our blunders, with flair and with care.

Cookies crumble, chips go crunch,
Belly laughs emerge with every munch.
Forks dance with glee, plates' circuits unwind,
In this feast of friendship, joy's never maligned.

Soda fountains bubble, karaoke calls,
Jumping on chairs, none musically enthralls.
Yet amidst the chaos, connection is found,
In every wild hiccup, silly moments abound.

So raise your glasses, let's toast to the cheer,
With every odd story, we indulge in the beer.
Our banquet of bonding will never grow old,
In the crumbs and the laughter, the best tales are told.

The Aftertaste of Adventure

Map marked with snacks, the journey begins,
With chips in our pockets and laughter like wins.
From mountains of nachos to valleys of cheese,
Adventure comes rolling like a fresh summer breeze.

In taco towns, we find treasure untold,
Guacamole rivers, storytelling bold.
With each crunchy bite, and hot salsa thrill,
We savor our quest; it's a taste that won't chill.

Candy-coated cliffs where sugar bees buzz,
Chocolate streams flow, it's like magic it does!
Each twist and each turn leads to sweets galore,
The aftertaste lingers, we're hungry for more!

So grab your spatula, your forks, and your knives,
Unwrap every moment, as our spirit derives.
This picnic of laughter, we'll cherish, you bet,
In the aftertaste of adventure, no regrets!

Ingredients of Insight

A sprinkle of doubt, a pinch of good cheer,
Mix in some wisdom, let's taste what is near.
Sauté all your fears in a pan of delight,
The simmering questions will cook up just right.

Stir in some courage, let it bubble and rise,
Flavors of laughter, oh how they surprise!
Serve up your heart with a generous scoop,
Invite in the joy, create a fun group.

Baking insights with might, adding sprinkles of chance,
Watch as they dance in a savory trance.
Douse with good humor, a dash of surprise,
In this kitchen of dreams, every cheer multiplies.

So whip up your dreams, don't fear the odd task,
Invite in the chaos, no need for a mask.
The ingredients of insight blend freely and bold,
With every sweet moment, more stories unfold.

Chew on This!

Bite-sized chunks of curiosity served,
Savor the flavors, no need for reserve.
Each chomp brings a question, a giggle, a smile,
Let's munch on the mischief, let's linger a while.

In the bakery of banter, fresh goods on the rack,
Giggling over donuts, as we twirl in the back.
"Why does the cake always look so surprised?"
With frosting-smudged faces, no wonder we're prized!

Grab a piece of the puzzle, pop it in bread,
Conversations rise high, like soufflés we spread.
A slice of this moment, a morsel of fun,
As we chew on this life, our hearts weigh a ton.

So whip out your forks, let's dig into bliss,
Every crunch tells a story, another sweet kiss.
We relish in laughter, life's banquet we miss,
So chew on this wisdom, it's hard to resist!

The Crust of Curiosity

Why do we ponder, just to know,
If cheese on crust is the star of the show?
With toppings so funny, they'll make you laugh,
And questions persist like a half-eaten half.

Should I add pepperoni or go with the green?
Will my dinner smiles cause a scene?
With every slice, I weigh my fate,
Savoring choices on my dinner plate.

As the oven hums with a cheerful note,
I ask my pizza, 'Did you bring a boat?'
With a wink of cheese and a wink of spice,
Life's funny moments are served with a slice.

So here's to the crust that holds it all,
To the crust of curiosity, standing tall.
In every bite is a question and jest,
Snacking away, life's wonderful test.

Artful Appetizers

Tiny bites on a flickering tray,
What's this mix of tastes and dismay?
With olives and cheese, they dance and play,
Is it art or a meal? Who's to say!

I munch on a cracker, it crumbles with pride,
While asking myself, 'Did I eat, or just hide?'
Garnished with dreams and a sprinkle of fun,
Each morsel I taste makes me feel like I've won.

So dip your bread in the sauce of delight,
As we ponder the wonders while taking a bite.
A sprinkle of laughter, a dash of cheer,
Appetizers of brilliance, how could they disappear?

In this banquet of questions, let's chat and cheer,
For artful appetizers bring friends ever near.
With every small nibble, a smile we'll share,
Snack through the chaos, savor the air.

Simmering Solutions

In the pot of wonder, questions brew,
Simmering left-overs and whims too,
Shall I toss in humor, or sprinkle some stress?
The recipe's wobbly, but I must confess.

A dash of mischief, and a blob of care,
Does it need more laughter? I stop and stare.
Stirring the sauce, I ponder the strife,
If only the answer could taste like my life.

With herbs of wisdom and spices of jest,
I toss in the flavors that feel like the best.
Shall I serve it warm? Or cold in a bowl?
These simmering solutions fuel every soul.

So here's to the kitchen, the heart of the sphere,
Where questions bubble and answers appear.
With each stirring moment, we gather and cheer,
For laughter and snacks are the best souvenir.

The Savor of Sentiment

A bite of nostalgia with every crunch,
Sentiments bubble, so let's have a bunch!
What flavor of memory tickles your tongue?
As we chew on the past, new songs will be sung.

An apple pie whispers of grandmothers' hands,
While chili reminds us of warm summer bands.
Holding our goodies as stories unfold,
The savor of moments worth more than gold.

With pastries of peace and cakes full of cheer,
Each morsel collects all we hold dear.
So let's feast on the stories, the flavors, the tears,
In this banquet of laughter, we toast with our peers.

For every sweet bite, our hearts intertwine,
In this savory journey, we rise and we shine.
So savor the sentiment in every delight,
As we share our snacks 'til the stars shine bright.

The Glimmer of Discovery

In search of answers, snacks in tow,
I ponder puzzles, where do they go?
A crumbed delight, a shiny treat,
Like bright ideas, they can't be beat.

With every bite, a new thought found,
Like pop rocks fizzing, joy's unbound.
The myth of steak, the lore of fries,
They spark the questions, no surprise.

From gummy bears to peanut bars,
My quest is sweet, beneath the stars.
I munch on chaos, nibble on fun,
Each savory lesson, a tasty pun.

So grab a snack, let giggles burst,
In every morsel, seek out the first.
For in each crunch, a mystery hides,
In cheerful bites, the spirit glides.

The Spice of Inquiry

Curious cats chase crumbs and dreams,
They dip their paws in whipped cream streams.
A dash of laughter, a splash of cheer,
Inquiries linger, like snacks we hold dear.

Popcorn questions, light and white,
Like sparks of thought, they dance in flight.
With flavors zesty, and zestful minds,
We mix up answers, one-of-a-kind.

Chili flakes linger, tickle the nose,
Each bite reveals what nobody knows.
Sweet or savory, the fun's in the chase,
Like asking where all the socks from the place!

Add a pinch of whimsy, a sprinkle of grace,
In every inquiry, find a new face.
Life's better spiced, with laughter and snacks,
Each question a journey, no need for tracks.

Hidden Answers in Every Crust

Crusty mysteries, baking well,
Piecing together each tasty shell.
Beneath each topping, secrets lie,
Like mysteries waiting to say goodbye.

The cheese fondue of queries inside,
With bites of laughter, they slide and glide.
A cherry cobbler, a secret stash,
Each spoonful's giggles, a sugary splash.

Slicing the pie, the answers twirl,
Whisk them together, give joy a whirl.
Like crispy chips, sharing is grand,
So munch on the moments, hand in hand.

In every crust, a riddle blooms,
With flavors aplenty, the laughter zooms.
So roll out your thoughts, bake with delight,
In the oven of wonders, the future's bright.

A Recipe for Wonder

Take a cup of giggles, a dash of fun,
Mix in a whisk until they've spun.
Add sprinkles of joy, and bake it right,
Under moonlit kitchens, what a sight!

Questions simmer like a tasty stew,
Adding spice with every new clue.
A dollop of dreams, how sweet they sound,
In pots of wonder, magic is found.

Sautéing laughter, frying the doubts,
In every sizzle, the joy just shouts.
Season with chaos, chaos that's good,
Stirring it gently, just like you should.

So whip up a batch, let creativity sing,
In every flavor, there's joy in the spring.
For tasty concoctions let questions roam,
In every kitchen, we find our home.

Baked into Being

In the oven of dreams, we rise,
With cookies that melt, and pies.
A dash of humor, a sprinkle of fun,
In this kitchen, we've only just begun.

We debate with the bread, who's the best,
While the muffins just laugh, they know the rest.
Flour on our faces, laughter we share,
Whipping up chaos, with utmost flair.

The cake takes the crown, but who's keeping score?
Through frosting and sprinkles, we crave for more.
Each bite a riddle, each laugh a delight,
In this bakery brawl, we feast day and night.

So here's to the snacks that brighten our days,
In the oven of life, we'll find our ways.
With a pinch of joy and a spoonful of cheer,
Let's slice up the moments, and pass them near.

Musing with Morsels

A donut philosopher, round and wise,
Pondering life through sugary guise.
Do sprinkles have meaning? Oh, what a plight!
In this bagel debate, we munch and ignite.

The chips say, 'We crunch, therefore we are,'
As salsa spills wisdom from a glass jar.
Each morsel a question, each crumb a reply,
In this feast of pondering, we live and we sigh.

A taco says, 'Embrace all your layers,'
In a tortilla wrap, we dance with our prayers.
With guacamole smiles, we dip and we dive,
Amongst seeds of thought, we endlessly jive.

So with bites of laughter, we munch through the day,
In a banquet of musings, we find our own way.
Each morsel a giggle, each taste a surprise,
In this gourmet ramble, wisdom never dies.

Journals of Juxtaposition

In the pantry of tales, jars line the shelves,
Peanut butter ponders, and jelly just yells.
Bread looks at butter, a spreadable fight,
In the chronicles of snacks, who gets the first bite?

Each flavor contemplates, in contrast they dwell,
The nachos all whisper, 'We're under a spell!'
While fries argue loudly, 'We're the true gold!'
In this dialogue of taste, each story unfolds.

Chocolate debates with a vanilla cone,
They squabble and giggle, never alone.
Popcorn pops wisdom, with a buttery cheer,
In this juxtaposition, snacking draws near.

So grab a fork, bring your wit to the table,
Each bite holds a chapter, each snack—its own fable.
In the journals of munching, we savor the prose,
With flavors colliding, the narrative grows.

Nourishment for the Soul

A salad whispers soft, 'Lettuce be friends,'
As croutons chuckle, their crunch never ends.
In this bowl of greens, dilemmas arise,
Tossing in laughter, a feast for the wise.

Hotcakes stack high, syrup drips like dreams,
In the breakfast buffet, nothing's as it seems.
With bacon debates and eggs on the side,
In this morning banquet, our joy cannot hide.

The smoothie sings sweet, blending hearts with might,
In a whirlwind of colors, we sip day and night.
Fruit-flavored secrets, like confetti they fly,
In this blender of moments, we reach for the sky.

So gather your snacks, as we dance and we twirl,
In this banquet of life, let the flavors unfurl.
With a spoonful of laughter, and a sprinkle of glee,
Each bite is a journey, come snack along with me!

Flavorings of Fate

In the pantry of dreams, we explore,
With pickles and candy, forevermore.
A dash of regret, a sprinkle of cheer,
The recipe wanders, but never sincere.

A cupcake of hope, icing so bright,
Yet buried within, a fruitcake's fright.
Stirring confusion, an ol' kitchen chore,
The taste of the questions, who could ask for more?

With flavors of fate, we laugh and we scoff,
A spoonful of wonder, we'll never take off.
Whisking through moments, some sweet and some tart,
Each bite is a riddle, food speaks to the heart.

So raise up your fork, and dig in with glee,
For the taste of existence is quirky, you see.
The snacks might run out, but worry not, friend,
The laughter we share never actually ends.

The Joy Between Nibbles.

Between every crunch, a giggle doth spring,
A symphony resounds when you munch on a thing.
Cookies and questions, a feast for the mind,
In laughs we discover what's often hard to find.

Nachos of wisdom, with salsa on top,
A dip into laughter, we'll never stop.
Every bite holds a secret, some savory, some sweet,
In between, we dance to the rhythm of eat.

Chips of delight, with a side of mirth,
Between each strange craving, we ponder our worth.
A platter of riddles, we savor the fun,
In bites of absurdity, we're never outdone.

So let's toast to the snacks, our edible dreams,
Each portion ignites inventive extremes.
In the joy found in nibbles, we gather and swirl,
For laughter and snacks make this world a whirl.

Whispers of Existence

In the fridge of infinity, secrets reside,
A mustard jar filled with truths we can't hide.
Like lettuce leaves rustling in warm summer air,
Each topping a whisper, a story to share.

The cheese has opinions, the ham likes to joke,
While pickles engage in deep thoughts as they soak.
With forks we unearth what's hidden from view,
In the salad of being, both funny yet true.

Lettuce is leafy, so wise and profound,
Yet tends to go limp when there's no one around.
The fruit in the bowl sings a tune all its own,
In flavors we twist, we never feel alone.

Let's feast on the nonsense, each bite brings delight,
In whispers of meaning, through day and through night.
The snacks may be fleeting, but laughter's a treat,
In the banquet of wonder, we savor and eat.

Crumbs of Curiosity

Tiny crumbs gather like thoughts in a heap,
Each morsel a question, too jumbled to keep.
What's under the lid of this cookie surprise?
Unravel the mystery hidden in guise.

A bite of the mundane, a nibble of cheer,
Exploring the options, we munch without fear.
With each cracking crunch, our minds take to flight,
Chasing the answers in the soft twilight.

Stale bread has wisdom, it's seen so much toast,
And whispers of stories worth sharing the most.
Each crumb left behind is a clue in the game,
Dissolving inquisitiveness, never the same.

So gather the snippets, let laughter be king,
In crumbs of curiosity, find joy in the swing.
Embrace every scrape, every fragmented delight,
For in culinary quests, our spirits take flight.

The Banquet of Being

In the kitchen of fate, we stir and blend,
Chasing flavors and smells, around each bend.
The recipe's secret? A pinch of cheer,
In every banquet, there's laughter near.

A banquet of dreams laid out on the plate,
Some dishes are odd, but we still celebrate.
With forks made of joy and spoons of delight,
We feast on the moments, from morn till night.

Between sips of wisdom and bites of fun,
We toast to the journeys that each has begun.
Radishes dance while the carrots sing,
In the feast of existence, we savor everything.

So raise up your glass of the fizzy sublime,
To the banquet of being, let's relish our time.
For here in the madness, the silly is king,
And life tastes much sweeter when you add a zing.

Craving the Unknown

A craving for wonder, what could it be?
Hidden snacks and surprises await you and me.
Do cookies count as wisdom, or pie as a guide?
As we nibble on questions, let curiosity ride.

The fridge holds the answers, all chilled and neat,
With mystery sauces and old leftover meat.
A dash of adventure, a sprinkle of glee,
Dig deep in the depths—what's waiting for me?

Crunching on breadcrumbs, I wander and roam,
Tasting each trial, it feels like home.
The universe giggles, it knows what I seek,
In the pantry of dreams, no morsel is weak.

So let's feast on confusion, it's savory bliss,
With each bite of the unknown, life's a sweet kiss.
And when we discover what's hidden in there,
We'll savor the secrets, our laughter to share.

Bites of Enlightenment

Snack-sized epiphanies pop in my mind,
Wrapped in bright packaging and sweetly defined.
With each little morsel, a lesson unfolds,
In the flavors of knowing, the universe holds.

Chocolates of wisdom, so rich and divine,
Sprinkled with humor like fanciful wine.
Each bite brings a chuckle, a giggle, a sigh,
Awakening senses as ideas fly high.

Cookie crumbs scattered like stars in the night,
Dancing through wisdom, they shine oh so bright.
With doughnuts of patience and pastries of cheer,
We feast on enlightenment, delicious and clear.

So munch on the insights, and snack on the truth,
With sprinkles of laughter, we savor our youth.
For in tasty revelations, we find in the end,
The sweetest of learnings, our dearest friend.

Sunset Reflections

At dusk when the sky is a canvas ablaze,
We dine on the colors, caught in a haze.
With crackers of hope, smeared in delight,
We snack on the moments that fade into night.

The sun winks down, with a twinkle and grin,
Pouring syrupy orange, let the feasting begin.
Each shadow a story, each cloud a new face,
As we gather the memories to savor and chase.

Chomp on the last rays before they retreat,
Stir up the giggles with each tasty treat.
As night tiptoes in with a whispering breeze,
We toast to the sunsets that gather like leaves.

So come share your laughter, your bread and your tales,
With desserts full of dreams, where adventure prevails.
For in every sunset, as colors collide,
We munch on the stories that swell up inside.

The Flavor of Wonder

In a land where odd things grow,
Lemon trees with purple snow.
Fridge whispers secrets in the night,
Pizza slices take to flight.

What's the quest, O hungry soul?
Finding snacks that make you whole.
Ice cream mountains, cake lake gleams,
Tacos whisper of sweet dreams.

The chips crunch secrets, loud and clear,
Popcorn kernels draw us near.
With every bite, a chuckle beams,
Food's a canvas for our dreams.

So here's to snacks with silly grace,
That tickle tastebuds, embrace space.
In this feast of laughing cheer,
Find your wonder, grab a beer!

Snacking on Uncertainty

Grapes dressed up in party hats,
Pasta asking where it's at.
The fridge is full, but what's the plan?
A dance with snacks, a funny scam.

Waffles stacked up like a tower,
Syrup rivers, tasting power.
Crispy chips in a rogue parade,
Confusion reigns but snacks don't fade.

Carrot sticks in deep debate,
Trying hard to find their fate.
Do they dip, or do they munch?
Oh, explore this silly lunch!

In a world where choices blend,
We snack on questions, not pretend.
With each bite, a laugh shall flow,
Uncertainty makes our munchies grow!

Pondering in the Kitchen

In a kitchen where giggles reign,
Pots and pans have much to gain.
A bubbling stew of jumbled thoughts,
Mixing flavors, tying knots.

A dance of spoons, a waltz of bread,
Spices winking, filling heads.
Questions simmer in the heat,
What's for dinner? Oh, a treat!

The teapot whispers tales of yore,
While muffins rise and dreams explore.
Taffy stretches on the floor,
Each sticky bite's a quest for more.

So take a seat, enjoy the show,
In this kitchen, wonders grow.
Amidst the laughter, cooking zest,
We snack on joy; we snack the best!

Morsels of Truth

In a world of crumbs and giggles,
Even broccoli sometimes wiggles.
Snack-time whispers truths so sly,
Pie in the face? Oh my, oh my!

Jelly beans in wild array,
Confusing adults, all in play.
Carbs and laughter make us bold,
Each morsel wears a story told.

A peanut sat, contemplating fate,
While olive oil might lubricate.
Crispy bacon knows the score,
Each bite's a tale to explore.

So gather round, both young and old,
As every snack brings truth untold.
In crumbs and giggles, we unite,
Morsels of joy, divine delight!

The Flavor of Existence

Woke up this morning, I pondered deep,
Is breakfast worth it, or just a leap?
Bacon dances on my plate so fine,
But is it just a riddle or a sign?

Syrup flows like thoughts in my head,
Pancakes stack high, where's my thread?
Maple whispers secrets sweet and bold,
Yet I'm still here, not finding gold.

Coffee brews like a nightmare spree,
What's the purpose of this next cup for me?
Each sip a question that sparks a craze,
Or is it just a caffeine-tinged haze?

So I munch on toast, in deep reflection,
What do I want? A hearty connection?
As crumbs fall down, humor takes flight,
Maybe it's just snacks that feel right.

Meals in the Midst of Mysteries

In the kitchen, a conundrum brews,
Leftover noodles, or something I choose?
Tacos or pizza, a noble debate,
The spice of decisions, just can't wait.

Do I want something sweet or quite savory?
Conundrums abound in culinary slavery.
Chocolate or chips, I need to find sense,
But all I find is a snack recompense.

Salad sits there, it's feeling ignored,
While popcorn dances, it's fully adored.
What's the meaning in this food circus show?
Maybe the answer lies in nacho cheese flow.

As I graze through scraps, with each little bite,
Life's mysteries blur, but snacks feel so right.
So when in doubt, just open a bag,
For joy awaits in every snack wag.

Cravings for Clarity

Questions arise like steam from a stew,
What to have next, a taco or two?
Scrambled eggs chirp, and pancakes sigh,
And suddenly I'm caught in a pie in the sky.

Do donuts hold wisdom? Are fries the key?
Every dish whispers, "Come dine with me!"
A feast of enigmas lying on the grill,
With every bite taken, I hunger still.

Chips crunch philosophically, say "Snack!"
Answers are tasty, when you're not looking back.
Lost in the layers of pizza so grand,
What's the secret? Maybe a slice in my hand.

So I dig into crumbs, watch the chaos unfold,
In the dance of the dinner, mysteries told.
With chocolate for wisdom, I find my way,
Through the meals and the madness, oh what a buffet!

Nourishment of the Soul

Each meal a riddle, each snack a quest,
Food for thought, who can eat the best?
Is a bowl of cereal a deep-life pit?
Or just a breakfast that tastes like a hit?

In the fridge, there's a leftover spell,
Some cheese that's wrinkled—who can tell?
A sandwich of questions, with mayo inside,
Is clarity lurking, or just mustard pride?

A mystery burger, with sides of despair,
Topped with a pickle, that's raising my hair.
But with every bite, I'm closer to truth,
Even crumbs of reckoning, a fountain of youth.

So I laugh and I munch, and dance on my feet,
Each snack is a giggle, life's joy bittersweet.
For in each little morsel, wisdom shall dwell,
In this feast of the foolish, I'm fitting in well.

Nibbles of Knowledge

In the pantry of thought, snacks reside,
Wisdom wrapped in foil, take a bite!
Crunchy questions dance in my mind,
Chewy answers are hard to find.

A cookie's crumbs guide my way,
While chips of insight lead astray.
Dip your fears in guacamole green,
Snicker at doubts like they're unseen!

Bite-sized truths, oh what a tease,
Each morsel prompts a giggle or sneeze.
What flavor of doubt do you choose today?
Cake, pie, or a handful of clichés?

So munch on your queries, feast on the fun,
Savor the nonsense till the day is done.
For in every nibble, a giggle's concealed,
In every morsel, a thought is revealed.

A Side of Wisdom

With a burger of hope and fries of despair,
I order a side of wisdom to share.
A milkshake of dreams thick and sweet,
Served in a glass, can't be beat!

I sprinkle some laughter on every bite,
A dash of humility makes it just right.
Life's kitchen is messy, with spills all around,
But the flavors of joy are easily found.

A crunchy pickle of folly on the plate,
Reminds me that bravery can sometimes wait.
Carrots of honesty crunch loud and clear,
While potatoes of doubt vanish in fear.

So let's feast together on platters of cheer,
Each bite a reminder, I hold dear.
Gather 'round tables where silliness reigns,
With seconds of laughter, all worries remain!

Echoes of Yesterday's Meals

In the fridge of memory, leftovers hum,
Grinning at dreams and old thoughts that come.
Yesterday's dinner still lingers in sight,
A casserole of hopes baked way too tight.

I can taste the regrets, like burnt toast on bread,
A soup of old choices starts to thread.
But a slice of today's pie is calling me near,
With toppings of panache, it's quite the career!

So I toast to the past with a fizzy old drink,
Each sip full of laughter and time to think.
For every hiccup is worth a good snack,
To savor the echoes and never look back.

In the banquet of yesterdays, we all start to see,
The flavor of wisdom is spicy and free.
So let us all dine on experiences dear,
And toast to tomorrow with a hearty cheer!

Forks in the Road

At each fork in the road, I pause for a bite,
Deciding if I'll travel left or right.
One path has sweets, the other is savory,
Should I munch on a scone or a tasty pastry?

A fork made of laughter must guide my way,
With whipped cream dreams to brighten the day.
I mix in some giggles with every small snack,
And whenever I stumble, I just bounce back!

With breadcrumbs of thought spread out on the ground,
I nibble and ponder what's yet to be found.
Chocolate rivers or a trail made of cheese?
Each choice, a delight, brings me to my knees!

So embrace the adventures laid out on your tray,
No wrong or right, just toppings of play.
Take a fork in the road, let your taste buds decide,
For every choice is a flavor, with joy as your guide!

Between Bites and Epiphanies

Chewing thoughts like gum, stretch wide,
A hidden truth with each bite stride.
Should I ponder or just indulge?
Choices haunt like yogurt's bulge.

Snacks parade on a plastic tray,
Do I munch or throw thoughts away?
Philosophers argue, crumbs in hand,
Who knew wisdom could taste so bland?

Crispy chips whisper deep and grand,
Yet nachos call, I just can't stand.
A question pops like popcorn's core,
Should I snarf it or seek for more?

Laughter bubbles with each new crunch,
The dinner bell rings, it's time to munch.
As answers dance on my plate of fries,
I'm realizing snacks hold the wise.

A Tapestry of Taste and Thought

Stitching flavors with a fork and knife,
Each sprinkle of salt reflects on life.
A savory blend of joy and dread,
Jellybeans tangle in my head.

Between the sips of fizzy drinks,
Epiphanies land quicker than links.
Do I savor or swallow it whole?
An open bag takes a hefty toll.

Cookies crumble with a side of doubt,
In smooth peanut butter, truths sprout out.
What lies beneath each crispy bite?
Starry visions on a pizza night.

Ultimately, we feast and jest,
Searching for answers, life's little quest.
With every nibble, I laugh and sigh,
For wisdom's dessert is a tasty pie.

The Dilemma on My Plate

At breakfast time, a strange debate,
Is syrup sweet or just too late?
Pancakes stack like questions high,
While bacon sneers, rolling an eye.

Lunchtime whispers, the tuna's bland,
Do I dive deep or take a stand?
The salad shouts with leafy glee,
Yet fries are calling, loud as can be.

Dinner's here, the fork feels heavy,
Did I bake patience, or just be chevy?
Sauces swirl like thoughts in flight,
As forks clash, I search for light.

With each course, the laugh lines grow,
The answer's simple, it's all for show.
In bites and laughs, my queries fade,
Joy is found, not in plans we've laid.

Forks in the Road of Understanding

Two paths diverged in my lunchbox wide,
One leads to salad, the other fried.
To chew on thoughts or taste delight,
Decisions spin like a dizzy kite.

Carrots crunch in a thoughtful guise,
But nachos wink with cheesy sighs.
Do I snack profound or simply snack?
The chips whisper secrets I can't track.

Sipping soup brings wisdom's grace,
While cookies simply quicken the pace.
Forks in the road ask me to choose,
Oh, what a pickle, I'm bound to snooze.

In a swirl of bites, confusion reigns,
As laughter bubbles, tickles my veins.
Snack away guilt, let folly unfold,
In the world of munching, truth is gold.

A Plate Full of Possibilities

There's a plate with a mix, oh so bold,
Fried pickles and donuts, or so I'm told.
A salad might sit, trying hard to fit,
While chocolate chips leap—aren't they a hit?

What's a bite without joy sprinkled around?
Each flavor a question, in taste it is found.
But when the plate spins, what should I choose?
Everything's tempting, it's quite the good news!

With taco conundrums and sushi surprise,
I ponder my options with wide-open eyes.
The crunch and the munch, a whimsical dance,
With every new flavor, I give it a chance.

So here at this table, with forks held up high,
I tackle the platter, oh me, oh my!
Each morsel a riddle, each dip a delight,
Let's savor this banquet, it feels so right!

A Taste for Truth

In the fridge there's a mystery, so big and so bold,
Leftovers whispering stories untold.
A sweet honey glaze, or some stew from last week?
The truth lies beneath, or so I should seek.

But why does the ketchup always seem stuck?
And why is the soup such a runny ol' muck?
I take out the pickles, and what do I see?
A salad has sprouted! Quite shocking to me.

Each bite a reflection, a nugget of thought,
What's wrong with a snack? Hey, it's all that I sought!
The chips provide wisdom, the cheese has a plan,
Together they whisper, "You're doing just grand!"

So here in this moment, a fork in my hand,
Truth tastes like pizza, quite perfectly planned.
With every fresh crunch and each savory slice,
I'm feasting on questions, and isn't that nice!

The Dessert of Doubt

A cupcake is waiting with frosting so bright,
But my gut says, "Maybe, just wait for tonight!"
With sprinkles of worry, and chocolate meltdown,
I contemplate choices while twirling around.

The cookie, it beckons with crumbs in the air,
Reminding me gently that sweetness is rare.
But doubting the frosting, so rich and so thick,
Has me asking myself, "Should I take a quick lick?"

Whipped cream on top feels like hope in a swirl,
Doubt dances in circles, it starts to unfurl.
What's life without sugar? A riddle, you say?
Yet I ponder the flavors, delayed by my sway.

So here on the plate, with a fork standing by,
I dive into dessert; oh, who needs to be shy?
For the sweetness of doubt, like a cherry on top,
Is better with laughter—let's savor, don't stop!

The Full Course of Questions and Quests

A soup full of wonders, so warm and so bright,
It asks, "What's the meaning of broth in the night?"
With noodles like dreams swirling here and there,
Each sip is a riddle—do you even care?

The salad arrives, crisp and full of its pride,
With greens like great wonders, I cannot decide.
The croutons are whispering, "Pick us today!"
While dressings debate, in a zesty ballet.

But wait, there's a roast, with a story to tell,
Tales of spices and secrets, oh do share as well!
Stuffing inquires, "Is my purpose just side?"
While gravy interrupts, like a sauce full of drive.

As dessert takes the stage in a sugary spree,
Cream puffs and tarts join the whimsical glee.
In this full course banquet, with laughter and jest,
It's questions and quests that we savor the best!

The Appetizer of Awareness

A slice of cheese, a curious thought,
Do I need it? Or is it just what I bought?
Crunchy carrots pepper my day,
With every munch I find my own way.

In a bowl of questions, I dip my fries,
What's it all mean? Oh, surprise!
Dip in some laughter, add a dash of zest,
Eating my doubts, I feel quite blessed.

Pickles and pickles, oh, where do they dwell?
A briny taste of a joke I can tell.
With each bite I puzzle, giggle and grin,
Snacking on wonder, let the fun begin!

Forgotten napkins promise sweet fate,
Tangled in mysteries served on my plate.
Nibble on wisdom, watch crumbs fly,
In this feast, the questions wave goodbye.

Chewing on Mysteries

What's the flavor of this grand old mess?
A hint of confusion, perhaps some duress?
Biting through layers of what I perceive,
Chewing on riddles, oh, I can't believe!

A cupcake of chaos, so frosted with doubt,
Take a big bite and just scream and shout!
The cherry on top, a silly surprise,
With frosting that sparkles and giggles and sighs.

Chomping on questions with jelly-filled joy,
What's behind that glaze? A philosophical ploy?
With sprinkles of humor, I take a deep breath,
Munching on life, ignoring old death.

In the end, it's a buffet of dreams,
Served with a side of bursting light beams.
Stuffed with the laughter, we'll dance and we'll play,
Chewing through mysteries, in our own funny way.

Savory Secrets of Existence

A cookie of wonders, fresh from the pan,
What's in this dough? A magical plan!
Each bite revealed, a secret or two,
Nibbling on truths like a pastry chef's brew.

Sautéed questions dance on my plate,
Is this the answer? Or just a new fate?
Spices of laughter, they tickle my tongue,
As I munch through the cosmos, forever young.

Soups filled with ponderings, warm and divine,
Each spoonful a mystery, all I can dine.
Like a wise old sage, I sip and I slurp,
Finding joy in the chaos, forever a chirp.

In every sandwich, a story unfolds,
Wrapped in the lettuce, the truth often holds.
Biting back doubts with every snack I attain,
Savory secrets reveal joy without pain.

A Spoonful of Solitude

A spoonful of silence, I savor, I dwell,
In the soup of my thoughts, oh, what a swell!
With croutons of comfort, I ponder and feast,
On the quietest moments, my very own beast.

A slice of solitude, served warm like pie,
Tastes bitter with questions, sweet in the sky.
Dipped in reflection, it dances in bliss,
Finds humor in shadows, in every small kiss.

A cupcake of calm in the chaos I live,
In each layer of frosting, I learn how to give.
Sipping my tea with a side of a grin,
Every pour revealing where troubles begin.

So here's to the morsels, both salty and sweet,
In solitude's kitchen, my thoughts find their seat.
A spoonful of relish, a dash of some fun,
In the banquet of quiet, oh how I have spun!

The Taste of Inquiry

Why do the cookies crumble so?
Are they laughing at me, not wanting to show?
The cake is quiet, a shy little slice,
Whispering secrets, oh, isn't it nice?

Do fries hold wisdom, drenched in their oil?
In the bubbling pot, do they plot and toil?
An onion rings out with layers of doubt,
Do they laugh when we cry? I have my route.

Bounce the dough, toss the pizza in air,
Is it a bird, or just cheesy flare?
A question of toppings; to you, what is best?
Let's top it with everything, what a grand fest!

Chips crunch their answers, in salsa they dip,
A playful little party, bring out the chip!
Beneath all the seasoning, flavor runs deep,
Chip on your shoulder? Just take a leap!

Answers on a Plate

What's the secret recipe on this tray?
Does the spaghetti dance? Is it here to play?
A meatball rolled away, a rogue on the run,
Eluding my fork—oh, this is such fun!

Green peas mingle, all round and so bright,
Poking a carrot, what a curious sight!
Do they plot together, this veggie brigade?
Making mischief, an edible charade?

The salad sings songs of vinaigrette dreams,
While croutons form clubs, or so it seems.
Beneath that dressing, is lettuce so sly?
Asking each question in a herby reply.

Dessert arrives in a sprinkle parade,
Brownies are winking, the cheesecake displayed.
Will I solve mysteries? Oh, where do I start?
With cookies that crumble, and pie that's an art!

Questions Beneath the Surface

What's lurking below in my golden fries?
Do they whisper tales of potato disguise?
With ketchup for courage, they hold a strong line,
As they dive into puddles, their fate is divine.

Why does the sushi roll make such a fuss?
Rice and fish partnering, creating a bus?
With seaweed so daring, it wraps up the tale,
While wasabi jumps in, the green little whale.

A bowl of cereal, oh what a riddle,
Why do they dance when I'm not being little?
A splash of cold milk, they sink without shame,
Yet float back to broil in the morning's great game.

What of the donuts, so round and so neat?
With sprinkles like stars, what a colorful feat!
They giggle in sweetness, confectionery kings,
Connected by laughter, and all of their rings!

A Feast of Epiphanies

Why does cake get the candles so bright?
Are they wishing for wishes, when they light the night?
With each flicker and glow, what secrets unfold,
As frosting whispers tales, sweet treasures untold.

The taco stands bravely with all of its might,
As salsa leaps forward, a zesty delight.
Who holds the answers wrapped tight in a shell?
With layers of flavor, it's hard to tell.

Beneath the pizza's crust, emotions collide,
Pepperoni feelings, can't let them slide.
With each gooey slice, a piece of the truth,
With toppings galore, we nourish our youth.

Oh, cookies and brownies, the laughter will soar,
With each little nibble, we always want more.
Bite-sized revelations come hand in hand,
In this glorious feast, we all understand.

Seeking the Satisfying

In a world of endless choices,
I ponder on what I crave.
Do I want the sweet or salty?
Or perhaps a mix to save?

With snacks like little puzzles,
I munch my way through clues.
Each bite a small adventure,
Do I like the red or blues?

The fridge hums like a chorus,
Each item sings its song.
I look for tasty wisdom,
Will my cravings steer me wrong?

Yet each nibble brings me laughter,
As I dance with cookie crumbs.
I chase my joy through flavors,
In this merry world of hums.

The Goodness of Questions

I ask the bread its secrets,
Does butter truly spread?
With every little inquiry,
I find snacks in my head.

Why's popcorn so exciting?
Why must chips be so loud?
Each crunch a tiny riddle,
In a munchy, crunchy crowd.

So many things to ponder,
As I feast upon a cake.
Do answers hide in frosting?
Or just vanish in a flake?

And in this quest for flavor,
I smile and laugh aloud.
For each question brings a smile,
In my snack-filled, happy crowd.

A Tasting Menu of Thought

I sit with plates of wonders,
On this thoughtful, tasty quest.
Carrots whisper life's meanings,
While cookies bring me rest.

With guacamole's wisdom,
And salsa's zesty cheer,
Each dip a chance to ponder,
As I snack away my fear.

A sip of fizzy laughter,
And fries that dance around,
Life's a buffet of questions,
With munchies all profound.

And as the flavors mingle,
I chuckle at the chance.
For every bite a lesson,
As I happily advance.

The Snack that Sparks

In a jar of nutty wonders,
I found a spark of fun.
Each clasp brings inspiration,
Just watch those ideas run!

With chips that crunch like laughter,
And sweets that dance with glee,
Each bite ignites a notion,
As happy as can be.

Popcorn popping with surprises,
A delightful little tease.
Will this flavor change the question?
With such tasty expertise?

In every nibble lies a story,
In every sip, a thought.
So snack and ponder with me too,
In the joy that life has brought!

Fragments of Flavor

In a cupboard far and wide,
I found some crumbs I tried to hide.
They whispered stories, sweet and salty,
Of moments lost, yet never faulty.

A jellybean from yesterday's feast,
Waged a war with a moldy beast.
They danced on tongues, oh such delight,
A comedy of flavors taking flight.

With chocolate chips that laughed and played,
Said, "We're here to make you be unafraid!"
A question asked, with laughter spun,
"Why not have chocolate? It's just plain fun!"

So here's my motto, sweet and clear:
Snack on joy, let go of fear.
Life's bizarre, a snack parade,
With crumbs of wit, a grand charade.

Baked Beneath the Surface

In the oven, a mystery brews,
A cake that sings and sometimes snooze.
It rises high, then takes a dive,
I giggle, thinking, "Will it survive?"

Flour flies like confetti in the air,
Sugar sneezes without a care.
Baking powder in a tizzy,
Making cookies that are kinda busy.

Why's the batter so thick and bold?
It had a secret, never told.
But with each stir, I find my quest,
To make this treat the very best.

I peer inside that golden dome,
At snacks which say, "We're not alone!"
Together they rise, a party grand,
In each bite, new flavors make a stand.

Wholesome Whys

What is this snack that looks awry?
A banana shape that made me sigh.
With peanut butter's smooth embrace,
I played detective, in this case.

"Why are you here? What's your intent?"
Said the apple pie with content.
"To bring you smiles, to make you snack,
And to sidestep worries on the track."

Grapes giggled hanging from the vine,
"Why not sip juice? It tastes divine!"
So here we are, a fruity crew,
A melting pot from colors' view.

So let the questions swirl and play,
With answers sweet, tucked in array.
Each bite a whimsy, laughter in tow,
Let's feast in joy, let worries go!

The Recipe for Discovery

Mix a dash of laughter with a pinch of zest,
Fold in some wonder, you'll craft the best.
Simmer your thoughts in a pot of cheer,
Serve up exploration, surprise is near!

Chop the onions of doubt, add garlic of glee,
Stirring the pot, it's just you and me.
A sprinkle of patience, a sweet, sticky time,
This concoction of chaos is truly sublime!

Bake it all gently at a cozy rise,
Watch as dreams melt, take your bite with surprise.
Don't forget the seasoning of playful debate,
In this feast of knowledge, let's celebrate fate!

So grab your apron, let's whip up a cake,
Of joy and confusion, make no mistake.
For every recipe's secret is found in the mix,
Just stir with a smile, that's the perfect fix!

Chewing on Choices

Biting into options, some sweet, some sour,
Choosing what to savor, oh what a power!
Do I want chocolate or maybe some pie?
Can't resist a cookie, oh my oh my!

In the buffet of chances, I take my stand,
A fork in the road, not sure what is planned.
Do I feast on fun or nibble on stress?
Each bite a decision, more or less!

A slice of confusion, a scoop of delight,
While pondering flavors, I munch through the night.
Tasty conundrums on plates so nice,
Will I find the truth in a bowl of rice?

So let's chew on our choices, one bite at a time,
Every flavor a riddle, every crunch a rhyme.
With giggles and juices, we'll tumble and roll,
For in every mouthful, we'll savor the whole!

Tasting the Infinite

With every bite, we ponder why,
A crunch, a munch, and wondering high.
Is this the start or just a tease?
A nibble of doubt, a bite of cheese.

We feast on dreams with mustard flair,
Juggling toppings without a care.
Pickles of wisdom, ketchup of fate,
This buffet's open, come grab a plate!

A sprinkle of laughter, a dash of fun,
Savor the moment, we're not yet done.
The soup of thoughts bubbles and swirls,
In this kitchen chaos, joy unfurls.

So let's toast the snacks, both big and small,
In this endless banquet, we're having a ball!
For every sweet that challenges our fears,
Is just a reminder: let's toast with cheers!

Rethinking Recipes

In a pot, a wonder stew,
Tossed in meats with a sprinkle of glue.
"What's that?" I asked, as things went plop,
A chili bean doing a happy hop.

Instructions read like ancient scrolls,
Mixed with giggles and a few trolls.
"Do we bake? Do we fry? Or do we munch?"
A potato chimed in, "Let's all have brunch!"

Cooking chaos, a wild ballet,
Where flavors clash and spices play.
The answer's clear in this pot of glee,
"Just toss it all, and let it be!"

A dish of laughter, a recipe grand,
Handed down from a stirring hand.
With each bite, let's question why,
And savor each snack as we all fly high.

Table Manners of Thought

Mind your manners when thoughts come to play,
Pass the salt of wisdom, hip-hip-hooray!
Chew on those ideas, both savory and sweet,
Table talk is messy, but oh, what a treat!

Sit down with your ponderings, forks all around,
Slicing through doubt on this table profound.
Take a bite of the strange while sipping on dreams,
Discussing the flavors of life's crazy schemes.

Wipe crumbs of confusion from the edge of your mind,
Make room for the humor, be friendly, be kind.
Invite all your worries, let them sit close,
In between slices of laughter, we boast.

So cheers to the moments, both quirky and bright,
With manners so funny, we'll feast through the night.
Raise your glass of ideas, let's toast to the fun,
In this banquet of thought, we're all number one!

www.ingramcontent.com/pod-product-compliance
Lightning Source LLC
Chambersburg PA
CBHW051656160426
43209CB00004B/918